John Bradley

Spontaneous Mummification

For Becky,
Fold along perforated
lines to make a
coronavirus mask!

love,
JC

SV

SurVision Books

First published in 2020 by
SurVision Books
Dublin, Ireland
Reggio di Calabria, Italy
www.survisionmagazine.com

ISBN: 978-1-912963-13-3

Acknowledgments

Grateful acknowledgment is made to the editors of the following, in which some of these poems, or versions of them, originally appeared:

The Bitter Oleander: "The Glue Between the States," "Just and Unjust," and "Placing a Mask of My Face Over My Face"

Calibanonline: "Again Let Us Begin"

Dispatches from the Poetry Wars: "View from the Moon"

Gargoyle: "Celestial Pablum"

Josephine Quarterly: "In the Pole of Cold"

Map Points: "Mission Statement"

The Night's Magician: Poems about the Moon, ed. Philip C. Kolin and Sue Brannon Walker: "Twenty Questions for the Moon"

The Poetry of Capital, ed. Clare Rossini and Ben Grossberg: "As Blood Is the Fruit of the Heart"

Sawbuck: "Dear Citizen Celan" and "O Novica, O Tadic"

SurVision: "Before My First, After My Last, I Wear Dirt's Shirt" and "Placental Gravity"

Thanks to Bonnie and Ric Amesquita, Mike Boughn, Marilyn Cleland, Joe and Jean Gastiger, Kent Johnson, George Kalamaras, Becky Parfitt, Susan and Christopher Porterfield. Thanks to James Tate for his kindness once upon a time in Alabama. Special thanks to Jana, who's kept me from spontaneously mummifying many times.

Mission Statement

Hereby let it be known: We chart our path like a dung beetle, rolling the future by the light of the Milky Way.

This book is dedicated to the dung beetle. Long may it roll.

Contents

Just and Unjust

The President finds a book, *Just and Unjust Wars*, on his Oval Office desk.

Without thinking, the President's hand reaches out to the book, lining its edges perfectly with the corner of his desk.

War is a people thing, he says to the book, *like a house made of zucchini, or a zucchini made from a dead horse.*

But with war, why haven't wild lions been brought before the court for crimes against human flesh? And why haven't judges yelled, Bring me the fields of poppies who are killing our people with their opioids? *Why?*

The President's forefinger taps the book several times, then listens to hear if anyone inside taps back.

After a battle, a soldier once told me he woke in a room filled with mushrooms.

Some mushrooms, they have many rooms, he told me, *so many rooms no one who has entered has ever returned.*

The President strokes the spine of the book, worrying a slight crease.

I could have been a great general, but I fall asleep at the sight of blood.

Placental Gravity

I was born in a box of Cheerios, inside the pantry, near the broom and
the bison.

I was born in my mother's armpit, her stubbly flesh smelling of a pickle
barrel.

I was born behind a common comma, mapping out the whirling world
of my coma.

I was breathing through the pores in my feet, pouring out a fog which
would later say, *Edgar Allen Poe poured whiskey on his
Wheaties.*

I was born with my head in my mouth, tongue in my brain, my blood
pounding this refrain: *All languages merge into a single
incomprehensible language.*

I closed my eyes, stars burning through my eyelids, so many stars I
knew they had to be ridden and riddle.

I closed my eyes, and I could see Walt Whitman humping a support
beam on the Brooklyn Bridge, Herman Melville in the
planetarium huffing whale blubber, Emily Dickinson in a black
veil scrawling her birth name on the belly of a tomato worm.

I was breathing through every line and stanza I had yet to write, words
floating just above and below the colon in my heart, telling me,
*Unbind yourself from the hands of the clock, even as the
numbers blister, as they snap, crackle, pop.*

I was breathing in all the cigarette smoke I would ever choke on,
mulching it into dead leaves.

My first words were *Hello, Placental Gravity. Hello, Slug in the Coffee
Can Soaking in Kerosene.*

My first words were *Everyone, take to your bomb shelter now. Leave
behind your welts and shredded wheat.*

I was, I was, and yet I was not yet born. This all happened when it will happen, only then and now.

No, I was born on the back of a velvet ant, wearing a tin crown. Laden with Lucky Charms.

The Glue Between the States

In Coral Gables, Florida, today, a man invented a new word for *knee.*

In Toledo, Ohio, a woman boiled a pot of green pea soup into a headache.

In San Diego, California, a retiree was found living in the back of the mouth of a former physicist.

In Poland, New York, a child located the Warsaw Ghetto in a sewer drain pipe.

In Bayfield, Wisconsin, a parrot said to its owner, *You may call me Thorazine, but don't try to call me Thor.*

In Galveston, Texas, small, jagged pieces of Maine were found in a ravine.

In Valley Stream, Long Island, a tongue escaped the mouth of a dog and was eventually found stuck to the side of a beehive.

In Bayfield, Wisconsin, a resident heard Lake Superior murmur, *My brain is almost transparent.*

In South Bend, Indiana, a loaf of rye bread settled at the top of a poplar. It had flown from a Panera in Portland.

In Wheeling, West Virginia, a crowd of crows dove into an open thermos of coffee. They have yet to emerge.

In Death Valley, California, a bird made of human and animal teeth was observed trying to eat a boulder.

In Cairo, Illinois, a piece of Asheville was found in a bowl of Froot Loops. No word yet of any dental injury.

In Moab, Utah, Thursday night invaded a home, sealed the windows and doors, and devoured all available electrical power.

In Pocatello, Idaho, a hair dryer was found plugged into a potato. It's been said to be running for at least twenty-nine days.

In Washington, D.C., a cracked cinder block was seen mating with the White House.

In Bloomington, Minnesota, a snowman entered the Mall of America and urinated on a small dog.

In Coral Gables, Florida, the new word for *knee* was just named the state bird song.

Whereas (1)

I breathe *allegro calmo senza rigore*, which means my legs rub
together calmly yet riotously.
I breathe the Declaration of Interstellar Sleep, though just hearing this
makes me drowsy, which makes me horny.
I breathe the bird nest baking in the oven, the ovenbird as it charts
unyodeled star formations.
I breathe forge and forger, forgotten and failing to forget, who sleep
undisturbed while sexual dirt asexually breathes.
I breathe tibias napping in a cradle, termites in my tomato soup,
wooden moles mating in a wordless mine field.
I breathe Ishmael, fishmeal, Babylonian email, erotic erratum.
I breathe undigested, undigestible word cloud, drifting in and out of
the visible.
I breathe a bucket of flammable eels, rivers that shed their skins each
moment.

While between each beluga-blue breath, someone near breathes
spontaneous mummification.

I breathe mint, mendicant, meridian, ambidextrous mummy, the
mound digesting a paper clip.
I breathe the desire to fall asleep at 11:11 in a car parked in the
Mississippi.
I breathe chairs made from heron breath, teeth made from crash
dummies, a heart made from a mouthful of mouth harp.
I breathe oud, cello, kazoo, igloo, hula hoop, hairpiece, ice pick,
macaroni, didgeridoo.
I breathe the sleep that perpetually wakes Sleepy John Estes.

Each breath with no memory of the one just before, no binding
contract for the one to come.
I breathe the unforetold, the untolled passed-back-and-forth-on-a-
levee-one-summer-night breath.
I breathe the roots dangling from *The Disambiguated Book of
Unconfigured Sleep*, my breaths rubbing together riotously yet
calmly.
I breathe unfettered through the many stomachs of you, dear
Morpheus, who has no need of breath, yet allows these lungs to
heave.

As Blood Is the Fruit of the Heart

As she was removing the shoplifting device from the white shirt.
As was required of her by the motion and mechanics of her job.
As the machine used to remove the device caught her finger.
As she knew her finger would bleed even before it bled.
As she didn't want blood upon the front of the new white shirt.
As she was holding a Band-Aid in her other hand to keep it ready.
As a long line of customers armed with clothing formed behind me.
As she paged Jason or Jennifer to come to the front desk now please.
As there can be no job without a Job no Job without a job.
As I didn't want to call attention to her act of inattention.
As I didn't want to insult the blood on the front of the white shirt.
As blood adores compliments but is easily bruised.
As it was her blood and not the store's or her supervisor's.
As she explained how some shoppers remove shoplifting devices.
As desire lurks in the blood no matter your zip code.
As I listened while she complained which made me complicit.
As I was a fellow bearer and lifetime spiller of that same fluid.
As I could always take the shirt back when it wasn't her shift.
As I didn't want her to be penalized for the action of her blood.
As no one should have to apologize for the suction of a job.
As ketchup or wine or olive oil would one day claim the shirt.
As I left the store with the small damp blotch on the shirt's whiteness.
As the shoplifting scanner by the front door did not detect fresh blood.
As blood contains beauty in movement but not beauty in stillness.
As I gently washed the shirt relentlessly with cold water and soap once
    home.
As blood calls for kindness even as it calls for erasure.
As I couldn't bear to wear a bloodstained shirt to the wedding.
As I knew my wife would see the blotch even before she saw the shirt.

As there is a drop of the moon's blood in our every article.
As there can be no sorrow no ecstasy without a thread of blood.
As blood is the fruit of the heart.

O Novica, O Tadic: Six Riven Sonnets

All history is in my body hair, every / bloody red atlas...
—Tomaž Šalamun, tr. Michael Thomas Taren & Tomaž Šalamun

1.

Anne Frank squats over an open book.
A goldfish stirs the mud in a cranium.
Stalin's grandson scrubs
his shadow's shadow's shadow.

O Novica. O Tadic.
O not quite invisible author.
O almost visible poem.
O most invisible reader.

Who can deny a poem without
breath, a ladder balanced
on the ass of a glass eye.

Someone with a potato for a head
speaks turnip to someone
with a beetle for a brain.

2.

Anne Frank wants out of this poem.
The goldfish wants out of its gill.
Stalin's shadow's shadow's
shadow burns a hole in his retina.

14

O Tadic. O Novica.
How can a poet be
a poet with the devil's
sputum in his mouth?

Should we talk Milosevic?
Talk Karadzic and Mladic?
Watch *Serbia's Got Talent*?

Translate Tomaž Šalamun into
doorknob stew, skull kinescope, cat
with a catbird's head.

3.

Poet zombies.
Construction worker zombies.
Hasidic Jew zombies.
Soccer mom zombies.

Only a sonnet can kill
a zombie. Though it would
also kill the living
and the unborn.

O Tadic, God is hungry.
You are hungrier.
You are angrier.

O God, Tadic is hungry.
Horny and happy
for a bowl of cold offal.

4.

Stalin's grandson reads this poem.
Stalin reads every damn poem.
Hungry not for poetry
but for poets.

O Tadic, in this sonnet
ashes of Anne Frank's
Frankenstein, made of barbed wire
and eggs and ashes.

Should we talk about the death
of the poem? The absence of silence?
Those little bells on your slippers?

Monster meaning
one who stirs moon milk moan
with the femur of a flea.

5.

To wake up with a potato
hole for a mouth and little potatoes
falling out of the potato-
making cavern.

The fork said to the heart
I'd rather be a spoon than a serpent
with a head for a tail
slithering inside some sonnet.

Where the word fevers.
Where it yellows and purples.
Where it shits hair and tooth.

Fattened and flattered.
O Tadic. The word spreads
its shapelessness across the moon.

6.

O the last sonnet will begin
with an O and end with a someone
who looks like Anne Frank
pushing a radioactive mop.

A poet is a worker and not
a poetic work. A poet is an imbecile
on meds who appears smarter
so much smarter when dead.

Anne Frank will not read this.
Stalin will read this and fart.
The moon will bleed through its pores.

O Tadic, the moon bleeds its gills.
Stalin drinks his grandson's urine.
Anne Frank scrubs the under floor.

View from the Moon

*Don't be afraid of anything. Nobody is going to do anything
to you.*
—Ratko Mladic, former general of the Bosnian Serb army,
to residents of Srebrenica.

Bits of shell and skull long-embedded in
my skin, I drag a dirty burlap bag
with some ugly hump inside. Could it be
Ratko Mladic, you wonder. That starfish

in my throat grows each time I extract it.
The world is a dirty burlap sack, says
Mladic. Unless he says, *Why would I eat
your foot when I could nibble your nipple.*

I'd rather teach an earthworm to read, but
ruptured blood salted the soil. *Why would
I amputate the head when I could leave
it there to fester*—Is *not* what I meant

to say. I'd rather wash your claw hammer
tongue. Melt your hammer with my tongue-washing.

*

Picture, if you can, a cloud at rest in
a house. A hand asleep inside that cloud
inside the house asleep in the head in
the cloud. This is when I open your skull,

18

replace the brain with mountain grass. A clutch
of ice. This is when I bathe your brain in
hydrogen peroxide, remove each word
that died and birthed another. This is when

I open the *Book of Soil* and spoon
feed it to the nearest root. *How far we
are from Schenectady,* you say. *Only
a piece of coal can cleanse the tongue,* I reply.

Knowing the word *pliers* should never be
spoken in the presence of tooth or tongue.

Dear Citizen Celan

This is the last such notice you will receive
as the possibility of a future cannot
with any certainty be sorely sustained.

We do not take delight in this, nor
deny some small basil taste of balm.

As with the cow with three udders
for a heart, and a rooster for an eye
and a crow for an eye

Citizen Celan, we possess no intention
of rending flesh from word, nor word
from flesh, or some combination
of the corporeally impossible.

A word—you know / a corpse
you once wrote, intending neither
to be funny nor unfunny, but
somewhere in the chasm between.

A dangerousness can be found in this

chasm, Citizen Celan, in the cracks leading
to and from. Those who have entered
and those who have exited

have never been delivered
from this region, as with the cow
caught in the colon in clear

violation of colon residency laws
yet retiring there as a cow in a colon will do.

Some things must be stored, some ravaged
some broken into smaller and smaller
breaks. As with the cow shattered
into winged piglets, each more
eyelid than wing.

It is this breakage,
Citizen Celan, this breakingness
unto brokenness that should
and should not trouble you.
That is, the aggregated calmness
and collision we refer to as you.

You may not always know
what has been done—or undone—
in your name,

Citizen Celan, but in your name
it was done, thus making you
complicit in it all. Though
some might plea, with ears

and eyes sealed, not guilty
due to near total ignorance
as with the unlame cow
with twenty-four chickens for a leg.

It is allowable to laugh here,
Citizen Celan, a small to middling

laugh conceivable, and as it is
permitted, therefore permissible.

We find nothing more can
or need be said. Thus ending
and erasing whatever may reside
or appear to respire here.

As with the eyes of the deer
inserted into the eyes of the cow
we reserve the right, at any time,
without warning, to partially
or fully revise you, our dearest

Citizen Celan.

In the Pole of Cold: List of Illustrations

A samovar is not a liquid coffin or spectral indwelling, 293

A shaman's liver teaching geese the exits of the human body, 14

A typical hair telling a neighbor what to do in the event of attack by the Arctic Ocean, 37

An ice floe demanding to be chopped into small, useful blocks, 3

Apologizing to a deer for removing its marrow, 119

As is obvious from the photograph, I once made this mistake and carried it with me wherever I went, 278

Baby born with iron teeth, 66

Below you can see the sun stowed inside an uncertain stomach, 124

Black and white ink blend in the Pole of Cold, 321

Chewing on caribou tongue, which he nightly conjured, 135

Far below the snow, you can see what it cannot, 63

Few still perform this three-day mating ritual upon the wheel of ice, 87

He swallowed a horse—not all at once—many times, 92

How often a pipe smokes the smoker's smoke, 183

I named this sled dog *Frozen Fish Arranged in a Crude Circle*, 39

I never ate a raw fish I hadn't first interrogated, 237

Inside this bird can be found a small iron stove, used by many a traveler, 72

It is necessary to believe whatever fits into an eel fits into an eel, 28

June sky pulling someone above or below the tundra, 237

Late at night, I could hear teeth being ground into flour, 22

Light given off by a clear egg that emitted no warmth, 377

Locals flavoring a corpse with the bark of a tree that is said to see only the right half of a visitor, 158

Locking a keyhole without a door, 321

No words can be eaten within the walls of this taiga church, 171

Pornographic pictures of the moon, 560

Said to believe only those who dip their tongue into a pot of boiling buttons, 349

Should you sleep upon a reindeer, you will not remember the manual of medicinal salt, 230

The skin of the white fox cannot be seen unless one has emptied his knife blade of all recorded sound, 98

Trace of global ennui, 392

The trouble with the sky, 488

This sled led me to a canoe, which led me to an axe, which led me to a bed, which led everywhere, 74

Unlocking a door without a keyhole, 44

Well heard by everyone: *White ink, black ink, on your right, on the left*, 123

What is the moon, after all, but a mail station without mail or station, 105

When night sticks to your hands, 83

Whether vanished or veinous, 116

Xyster alongside the inevitable tea window, 59

You, a luxury we were forced to shed, again and again, 251

Twenty Questions for the Moon

How is it I can fit the Nile River in an eyedropper
but not your delicious light? Spilling, plunging,
surging—which best describes the hunger of your
Sea of Fecundity? If I make a crooked circle
with forefinger and thumb, hold it up until it
surrounds you, will you blind me, or make me
surrender to wakeful sleep? On that plaza in Manaus
named for you? What was it Li Po said
when he sank into your long cadaverous arms?
Tell us, why is NASA hiding our kidnapped children
in colonies on Mars? Plunging, surging, spilling—
which best describes your vaporous white hair?
On that steep street in Galway named for you?
When Galileo gazed through his telescope
at your granulated flesh, how softly did he say,
I am made of moon and web and ravenous crumb?
Do you prefer being compared to a peeled lemon,
slice of unripe banana, or hammered tin head?
On that back street in Reykjavik named for you?
Is it true you keep a list of every fool
whoever mooned you? Surging, spilling, plunging—
how is it you shadow me by day, I shadow you
by night? O carnivorous moon, may I serve you
at the Banquet of Luminous Beings? On plates
of damp moonstone? With narcotic blooms
of moonflower? In Novosibirsk, near
the unfinished nuclear waste repository,
in the middle of the roundabout named for you?
What was it you told Li Po when he embraced
your surging, spilling, plunging arms? When

will we build a delirious wall to keep you
from seeping into our dream reservoir? Why
did you tell those moonstruck kids NASA kidnapped
and sent to Mars, *If you wear silver gloves*
no one will be able to withstand
the beauty of your vaporous hands?

Celestial Pablum

After Remedios Varo's painting of the same name

I must feed the moon, you say, as you turn
the wheel, grinding gelid night stars into ever
bright pablum. It's wrong, though, to consume
living light. *Nothing can be more right than riven salt,*
when silted with kindness, you tell the stars, as you grind
their shine into swirling powder on the small ceramic plate.
But you are captive here, Remedios, bound by
celestial task, punished for bringing edible light
into this inevitable world. *Stand back*, you warn.
Few can resist the shifting, sifted light. But why,
my lower back asks, why cage the curling crescent
moon? Soundless as moth crumb. Why forever
feed on its unending hunger? *I must follow this*
spoon, you note, *into the merest mouth. Even*
as it glows with the shine of skull. But why? Why not
let the moon glaze our flesh? Let it feast on vowel
of owl and vole. Silence. *I must feed the moon,*
you say, grinding the cosmos into dust.

For the Black Angel, Oakland Cemetery, Iowa City, Iowa

You call yourself Rodina: Rodina Feldevertova: but

I know your name: it's *Before You Worried Away*
Each Thumb: it's *When Misshapen Memory Is a Wing*
Rinsed in the Blackened Earth. I can give you

a penny: a pen: my sweaty perambulations. You

lookdown: away: back to where one day you'll
lead us: to the iron cradle filled with oranges:
still warm from the forge. What was it my father

wanted to tell me: each time in the motel room

when his soft voice: broke: all I could hear was
the rustle of your wings: newspaper singeing
your fingers. I wanted to shake you: shudder

you back into silence: the iron ore before gesture.

You say I fallow the words wrong. I don't know who
I'm saying: what I speak with. One day I'll pause
before a stranger without thumbs: and then whoever

I've stung: however wrong: will I come undone.

Before My First, After My Last, I Wear Dirt's Shirt

That shirt I buried belonged to my father, his lifespan of breathing dirt. I didn't care that the shirt would remain alive and alert in the dirt. Oh, to dig a shirt out of the earth and wear it for a little while above the dirt. It wasn't that the shirt had had relations with some malodorous dirt. I should let the dirt bury whatever it wants to bury in the dirt. *Dirt to dirt*, I said over the hole in the earth, *shirt to shirt*. As we all know, a shirt should never be worn by shapeless or even shapely dirt. I should never have listened to those holes eating the collar of the shirt. I buried the shirt because . . . because all around me there was so much dirt. I should not have let something that commingled with skin commingle with dirt. I don't really want to know what happens when dirt begins to inhabit a shirt. I've buried the ashes of a sickly cat, a contaminated book, but never a still breathing shirt. If only I'd listened to the sky and let the shirt expire in a tree like withered dirt. And if the shirt should rise up and flail its flimsy arms, flinging loose pebbles and dirt? Oh, to fall to the dirt and vanish at the same moment as your earthly shirt.

Franz Kafka on the Last Day, or When the Messiah Comes

*The Messiah will come only when he is no longer necessary; he
will come only on the day after his arrival; he will come, not on
the last day, but on the very last.*
–Franz Kafka

When the Messiah comes, Father
at the dinner table, will wash
his fingers in the fingerbowl
Mother filled with red wine.
From the bowl, each of us
takes one sip.

Mother will burp, and a family
of toads will arrive
from her mouth, telling us
of great rejoicing in her
internal organs.
Ottla shall stand, sit,
and begin to weep
quietly into her long skirt.

When the Messiah comes
Haile Selaisse shall writhe
in the streets, money
raining down upon all around.

In the country, sheep shall lose
their wool, and in its place
scales appear.

Snakes, shedding their skins,
will bear a white fur
much like pussywillow.

And every heart, on that day,
shall stop, for three beats,
then resume at the speed
the earth carries.
And all those who never bothered
to wear green shoes, they
shall be punished.
And all those who dared, even once,
to wear green shoes, they
shall not go unpunished.

*

When the Messiah comes, there
I shall be, at my writing table
writing out what is owed
to the laundress.
In the lamp's steady light,
bits of darkness.
And in the darkness around
the lamp, many lights.

A stocky man, much resembling
Father, bumps my door open
with his belly. Leaning in
the doorway, he picks his teeth, staring
into the empty space I have come
to occupy. Every act of cruelty
a god divined by love.

I dumbly gaze down
upon the advertisement in my lap
for a bar of bathery soap.
You will smell, it promises,
like Japanese haiku.
The horror of language
is words. They can be made
to say *anything*.

A flamingo, trapped within
the wardrobe, shakes
its wings. In the back,
huddled, I find you,
sister, afraid for us. To stop
your shivering I hold you close.

Is this, then, the Messiah?
you shall ask, Ottla,
on the last day, the very last,
when the Messiah comes.

Whereas (2)

I breathe Ten Sleep, Wyoming; Sleeping Bear Dunes, Michigan; Sleepy
    Eye, Minnesota.
I breathe Zoheth, Shearjashub, Beriah, Behuel. Amaziah, I breathe.
I breathe *allegro calmo senza rigore*, which means my legs rub
    together calmly yet riotously.
I breathe the ladder in my bed that breathes through my inner ear.
I breathe at the corner of Curb and Delay, Lunch and Divine, Mercy and
    Retrieve, in the Year of Boiled Sleep.
I breathe the dirt in my dirt shirt as it expands and expires, returns,
    respires.

I breathe, whenever possible, that little bit of infinity, whenever I
    breathe.
I breathe pulverized sleep cleaved back together at 9:41:41.
I breathe a baby with a gun humming its gums on an elevator with a
    lawyer in my spine.
I breathe lubricant zone, ethereal nostril, wall sealant, evening eyelid
    of a dreaming ant.
I breathe someone with a Milky Way accent, which means I linger too
    long in your left lung.
I breathe paring knife and collarbone long after you've gone to devour
    another breath.
I breathe Buster Keaton's bivalvular romance with Emily Dickinson, her
    suitcase full of chewed blueprints and bruised day lilies.

Breathe, Beluga-blue breath. Breath, breathe. Out of respect for
    infinity. Respect for spontaneous mummification.

Spin, hum, reject, inject.

I breathe the hiss of history long after the spoken reaches the sodden
and the sudden.

I breathe the roots dangling from *The Disambiguated Book of*
Unconfigured Sleep, my breaths rubbing together riotously yet
calmly.

O to breathe the breath of the gravedigger's cello, elbow to elbow. Is
and never was.

I breathe, I breath, I breathe underwater origami a bit lighter each time I
breathe.

I breathe unfettered through the many stomachs of you, dear
Morpheus, who has no need of breath, yet allows these lungs to
heave.

Placing a Mask of My Face over My Face

I aspire only to silence. I could not let you know
this I was told, and yet here I am releasing sounds
once stored miles below your shoe. Rules make me

want to run to a glass room, vomit a broom, and blind
each wall with dank river mud. I could say you will
stab my every exhalation and it will not harm me.

You will charm me and make me kinder and smarter,
lilting the tilt of the planet. I can't quite see the trace
of your face, yet I'm told it resembles a baggie of frozen

starlight, a shot glass of lung water, a vial of sea salt
vapor. I aspire only to invisibility, the skin around the rain
droplet on the back of your hand. I don't know you,

or I know you but don't yet belong to you, the slight
scar on your throat. I feel stronger, the rules flimsier,
after I've found in the corner, under the carpet, a slim

black turd. Perhaps you wish to smack me, so I'll glow
about the head. I'm never certain when you're in
the garage, engine running, what you grasp of desire.

That crescent moon only seen through the bottom
of a rusted bucket. Thus I leave you, listing with silence,
aspiring only to what shall be spilled.

Again Let Us Begin

In memory of Tomaž Šalamun

You, so afraid of disinterred lightning. Your libretto calls
for stilled sleep. Steeped salt. We drape this sheet over
what you unknowingly blink. Char and feather clinging
to collar, cough. Tomaž, you once opened a can of tuna fish
to fondle non-human flesh. To dandle what we crave.
Discorrect what we collect. For us you drew a god down
your bile duct to claw, speak, burr. Gnaw through the wall,
tonsil and toad. Vertical and blur. A smitten tinsmith hammers
inside someone's mouth. Leaving us this to stumble and chew.
Error and eros. We can always never fully unspool the end
of this world through finger or poem. Done again, let us begin.
Always ever. Though little remains but the longing for flesh
that cannot feather and char. Bray or abrade. Begin again.

When You Imprint onto My Back the Milky Way
(In 3-D, Please)

Be sure, at each turn, the Milky Way may endure my zonal flesh.
If you can, be sure of the unsayable, the inextinguishable.

The long-gone-to-unspun-rainmust surely be sure each element
of syllable and linger saturates *Under the cope of the moon*

and *Eat it and grow mad*. Moreover, be sure the embers cleanse
what is called the edible alphabet; cover it over with crack-in-my-
    skull

dust, which when inhaled brings the liver's lung ever further
into the goingness-unto-gone. Be sure, for you will be glad of it,

the belly and the like do not steal the ever-more-clear-brightness
from the intestinal polar region in the long turning. Be sure,
    moreover,

the Milky Way, in breathing iron and ocean, stammer and yaw, will
translate me far beyond the reach of unforeseen mummification,
    even

as another vehement heat will have found me. As you ingest this,
be sure joy is mingling about your middle, for the agitated will run

about the sky even as the sky grows amongst us ever more agitated.
And be sure, even unto the unsure, my once-a-green-lizard tongue
    speaks

to those bound to ankle, waist, neck, head, hair. Moreover, be
sure, even now, I breathe in every place the Milky Way does breathe,

which will, I know, break me. Burst me into silky, crumbling light.
Into *Let it abide*. Into: *So do all living creatures, knowing and unknown,*

venture forth wherever they roam, the Milky Way adrift on their back.

More poetry published by SurVision Books

Noelle Kocot. *Humanity*
(New Poetics: USA)
ISBN 978-1-9995903-0-7

Ciaran O'Driscoll. *The Speaking Trees*
(New Poetics: Ireland)
ISBN 978-1-9995903-1-4

Helen Ivory. *Maps of the Abandoned City*
(New Poetics: England)
ISBN 978-1-912963-04-1

Elin O'Hara Slavick. *Cameramouth*
(New Poetics: USA)
ISBN 978-1-9995903-4-5

John W. Sexton. *Inverted Night*
(New Poetics: Ireland)
ISBN 978-1-912963-05-8

Afric McGlinchey. *Invisible Insane*
(New Poetics: Ireland)
ISBN 978-1-9995903-3-8

Anatoly Kudryavitsky. *Stowaway*
(New Poetics: Ireland)
ISBN 978-1-9995903-2-1

Tim Murphy. *The Cacti Do Not Move*
(New Poetics: Ireland)
ISBN 978-1-912963-07-2

Tony Kitt. *The Magic Phlute*
(New Poetics: Ireland)
ISBN 978-1-912963-08-9

Clayre Benzadón. *Liminal Zenith*
(New Poetics: USA)
ISBN 978-1-912963-11-9

George Kalamaras. *That Moment of Wept*
ISBN 978-1-9995903-7-6

Anton Yakovlev. *Chronos Dines Alone*
(Winner of James Tate Poetry Prize 2018)
ISBN 978-1-912963-01-0

Bob Lucky. *Conversation Starters in a Language No One Speaks*
(Winner of James Tate Poetry Prize 2018)
ISBN 978-1-912963-00-3

Christopher Prewitt. *Paradise Hammer*
(Winner of James Tate Poetry Prize 2018)
ISBN 978-1-9995903-9-0

Mikko Harvey & Jake Bauer. *Idaho Falls*
(Winner of James Tate Poetry Prize 2018)
ISBN 978-1-912963-02-7

Tony Bailie. *Mountain Under Heaven*
(Winner of James Tate Poetry Prize 2019)
ISBN 978-1-912963-09-6

Nicholas Alexander Hayes. *Amorphous Organics*
(Winner of James Tate Poetry Prize 2019)
ISBN 978-1-912963-10-2

Gary Glauber. *The Covalence of Equanimity*
(Winner of James Tate Poetry Prize 2019)
ISBN 978-1-912963-12-6

Maria Grazia Calandrone. *Fossils*
Translated from Italian
(New Poetics: Italy)
ISBN 978-1-9995903-6-9

Sergey Biryukov. *Transformations*
Translated from Russian
(New Poetics: Russia)
ISBN 978-1-9995903-5-2

Alexander Korotko. *Irrazionalismo*
Translated from Russian
(New Poetics: Ukraine)
ISBN 978-1-912963-06-5

Anton G. Leitner. *Selected Poems 1981–2015*
Translated from German
ISBN 978-1-9995903-8-3

All our books are available to order via
http://survisionmagazine.com/books.htm